Looking at Music

by
Chris de Souza

VNR VAN NOSTRAND REINHOLD COMPANY
NEW YORK CINCINNATI TORONTO LONDON MELBOURNE

Stop and listen

The world is full of noises. Just open your window and listen to them all! Try and sort out all the noises from each other. Everything has its own noise which you can hear if you listen hard enough. Just as you can recognize a thing by its color and shape, you can also recognize it by its sound.

Noises are all different and you can sort them out in three ways. They are either higher or lower in *pitch* (think of the difference between a man and a woman talking); or they are longer or shorter in *duration* (for example, the difference between a car passing and a tap on the door); or they are louder or softer in *dynamic* (for example, a train passing nearby or one passing far away). Every noise you hear is a mixture of these three things: pitch, duration and dynamic.

Listen to all the sounds around you. Make a list of them, sorting them out into louder, longer and lower sounds or softer, shorter and higher ones.

How you hear sound

When you make a noise – for example, when you clap your hands – the air around your hands moves away in invisible waves. Although you cannot see this, the air around you is full of invisible movement, similar to that made by waves in water. Some of these air waves are sound waves. When the waves reach your ears, your ears turn them into electrical impulses which travel into your brain. Your brain acts like a computer, and sorts them out, telling you what sort of sound you are hearing. If it is too loud, your brain will make you cover your ears with your hands to protect them. If the noise is very soft your brain will tell you to cup your hand around your ear to help you focus the sound better. If the noise is made by something dangerous such as a car speeding straight at you, your brain will tell you to run out of the way.

Do you want to hear all those sounds coming in through your window? Are they agreeable or disagreeable? If you do not want to listen to them you can close your window and most of the sound waves will stay outside. But they will still make the window vibrate a little. The vibration will make the air in the room move around you and you will still be able to hear the sounds outside, although they will now be muffled. The window is like a breakwater in the sea: on one side the water is rough and on the other it is smoother and calmer. On one side of your window the air waves are strong, on the other they are weaker, unless you make a lot of noise in your room!

Organized sound

Well, with all that noise going on, why do we want music? After all, it is only more noise. But music is very different from the noise outside your window. The noise outside is confused and disorganized and can often be very annoying. Musical noise is organized and can be very pleasant. The difference between disorganized and organized sound is similar to the difference between a simple meal, such as hamburgers, and a meal which takes hours to prepare. Sounds

Low, long, soft

Low, long, loud

High, long, loud

have to be organized in order to become music, and they can have a very strong influence on you. They can make you tap your feet or dance, or march; or they can make you feel sad or sleepy. In this book you can see how people use music in these different ways. People who organize sounds are called composers. It is easier to compose music than you might think, but some people have composed music in such a special way that their music is listened to all over the world, sometimes hundreds of years later.

Composers imagine patterns of noises, or tunes, in their heads. Then, when they are sure how the patterns are made up, they write down a set of signs that tells musicians what instruments to play and how to make the special noise patterns the composers imagined. When we hear the sounds, we listen for the patterns the composers have invented, and these patterns affect us in different ways. If the composers are clever and use colorful sounds, they can excite us; or if they use complicated sounds, or sounds made purposely out of order, they can make us feel sad or thoughtful. In this book we will see how composers from the past and present have made musical patterns for us to listen to.

Some of the noises in this picture are described below. List others being made, saying whether they are high or low, long or short, loud or soft. Remember that quiet noises nearby sound louder than loud, distant ones. The ducks are making waves in the water similar to the way sound waves move in the air.

High, short, loud   **Low, long, soft**   **High, long, very soft**   3

Sound becomes music

On the previous page you found out that the world is full of noise and that music is organized sound. How did people decide what things to use to make their music?

Have you ever been doing something such as woodwork or gardening and suddenly found your hammer or spade making a particular noise which catches your attention? Well, that's how the first people probably started to make music thousands of years ago.

Prehistoric people first made tools out of stone, wood or bones, and much later with metal. Perhaps, when they were using their stone hammers, wooden spears or bone cups, they discovered the different noises they could make. Then it was not long before they used the noises their work-tools made to make music as they worked, and probably they sang, too. The beat or rhythm of the music would have made the work easier. As the centuries went by, they began to adapt their tools in different ways so that they would make specially pleasant noises. They discovered that different-sized clay or wooden pots made different sounds when they were hit, and that if they covered them with animal skins they made very good drums; seed-pods made good rattles. They discovered how to make hollow bones and reeds into pipes. In this way everyday objects that had started off as weapons or tools became musical tools or instruments.

From bow to harp
When men started to use bows and arrows perhaps they discovered that the string of the bow made a twangy sound. If the bow was tight, the twangy sound was high in pitch, a loose bow made a lower twang. Very soon they began to make a different type of bow just to play as a twangy instrument. The next step was to give it more strings so it could make a range of notes. However, the sound still did not have much power. Then people discovered that if they put a hollow piece of wood at the base of the bow, this would act as a *sound-box* and make the noise louder; the sound-box now forms part of nearly all string instruments. Soon the strength of

Above: The history of the harp.
a) A simple, one-stringed bow.
b) An Ancient Egyptian harp with more strings and a sound-box.

c) A model of an Egyptian harpist.
d) A medieval harp with a supporting strut on the third side.
e) A modern orchestral harp.

the strings on the musical bow became too strong for the wood and another piece of wood was added to stop the bow collapsing. This began the development of the modern harp.

Some early harps were discovered recently in one of the Egyptian pyramids where they had been buried with a king about 5,000 years ago.

On pages 20 and 21 you can see what some present-day string instruments look like. Of course, their sound-boxes are much more complicated than the early ones.

Steel bands

Nowadays people are very clear about what they consider to be a musical instrument. In fact, anything can be used as a musical instrument to make noise or music.

A recent example of the way a modern 'tool' has turned into a very exciting musical instrument is the use of the oil drum in the West Indian steel band. The workers in the oilfields in Trinidad used empty oil drums as musical drums. Very soon they found that they could make these oil drums play different notes by dividing the top of the drum into a pattern of different-sized shapes; each part of the pattern would make a different note when hit. By using many drums, they could play whole tunes.

Make your own steel band

There are probably many tools in your house that would make interesting instruments. Some composers have used anvils, saws and hose-pipes! Make your own steel band out of some empty cans. Make sure you ask an adult to help you first. Draw simple patterns on the bottom of each can. For example, you could divide the base into three different-sized segments. Put them over a gate-post or block of wood one by one and, with a hammer and blunt steel tool, tap along the lines you've drawn. When you hit different parts of the pattern with a hard stick they will make musical noises.

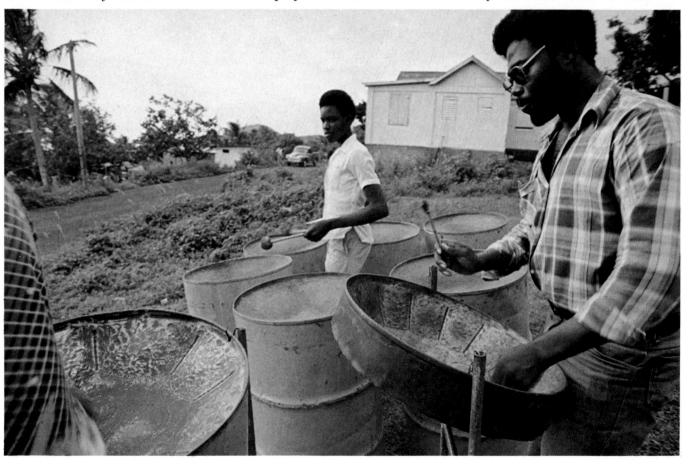

Above: A West Indian steel band. Can you see the different shapes that have been beaten out on the tops of the oil drums in this band?

The smaller shapes on the shorter drum (see right) make higher notes. Some of the big drums (see back) give only one or two

low notes, and two or three are used by one man. The player on the right can play a whole tune on his single drum.

The power of music

You have read how people used their instruments to make music while they worked and how the music helped them work. This is a good example of the power music can have. Primitive people in tribal societies today still use music to help them in their daily life. They have songs for walking, songs for playing – and music for making babies sleep! Perhaps the most common of all are working songs, such as those sung by laborers in Nigeria.

Can you imagine a world without music? The power of music is something everyone needs, though they may not always be aware of it. We have music wherever we go: in shops, cafés, churches, trains, planes and cars, in waiting rooms and wherever we can take our radios and cassette-players. Lively music may be used to make people work faster in factories; slow music can lull you into buying more cans of food in a supermarket.

Making magic

In many parts of Africa and the East, people have thought that music has magical powers, capable of healing illnesses and calling up evil or good spirits. Music is still used in this way in some tribes. A good example of the use of the power of music in a religious ceremony today is that of the Whirling Dervishes in Turkey. They whirl around and around for hours on end until they forget who or where they are, and they are in a complete frenzy. People do almost the same thing when they go to a disco. Loud music with strong, repeated beats acts on us like a drug: it sets our

Above: The Whirling Dervishes perform their ritual dance.

hearts and pulses beating faster and faster. It gets us to move in time, tapping our feet, or jumping up and down, and it helps us to forget our worries.

If this happens to a whole group of people at the same time, it has an even more magical effect. Everyone may feel happy to be together, or the music may make a whole crowd of people act like stampeding cattle. People get a thrill out of singing together at football games, for

Right: The Pipes and Drums of the Second Battalion of the Scots Guards march from the Wellington Barracks in London.

Left: Modern ballroom dancers
get a great thrill out of performing
on the dance floor.

instance. They also get excited by watching bands marching by in parades, and feel very proud as their national anthem is being played. Marches used to help people go cheerfully to the dangers of war, and funeral marches helped them get over the shock of losing friends and relatives killed in battle. Music helps religious services to be solemn or joyful. It also helps people feel more relaxed at parties.

National music
People in different countries have their own style of music to excite them. Dance music shows the different national styles very clearly. Some composers have used the tunes and rhythms of their countries' music in their own music to show how much they loved their own country. The American composer Aaron Copland (1900–) combined folk tunes and jazz style in his ballet *Billy the Kid* and in *Rodeo*, works that remind us of legends of the Old West at the same time as they have the sound of modern, even experimental music. George Gershwin (1898–1937) is another well-known composer who used jazz and classical styles to create uniquely American music. His folk opera *Porgy and Bess* is probably the most famous of his compositions.

Experimenting with sound

Look around any room in your home. You can probably find a great many objects which can make very interesting noises. Almost anything in a house can be used just to provide a noise! If you put a few objects together you can make your own very special type of band. You can arrange the noise-makers into different groups, depending on what they are made of (for example, wood, metal, pottery or glass) or how you make a noise with them (for example, blowing, scraping or shaking). You can bang wood together, blow across the top of bottles, rattle a can with buttons inside, or scrape pieces of metal together. If the object is made of glass or metal, the sound it makes when you hit it will probably be a longish noise, similar to a bell or gong being struck.

If you hang a metal object on a loose piece of string, the noise it makes when you strike it will last longer because there is nothing to stop the metal vibrating when you hit it. The vibrations make the air around the object move until the sound reaches your ear. If the vibrations are stopped, the noise will stop. Look carefully at the metal after you have hit it and you will see it shaking very fast; if you touch it with something soft, it will stop sounding because the vibrations have been stopped.

The noise anything makes also depends on with what you hit it.

Experiment with all kinds of different materials to see which ones make the most interesting sounds. Then make a list of the ones you like best, and why. It is great fun to make music in this way. It will not sound like 'normal' music, but it certainly is music because you have specially organized it for fun.

Organize your sounds

Now you can organize your collection of sound-makers. Decide which ones to sound, how you want them to sound, what other sounds to play with them, how long the sounds should last (*duration*) or how loud or soft they should be (*dynamic*). How

Right: To play this musical game you will need some playing cards and dice. Each color on the board stands for a noise. Give each noise-maker (examples are given below) a separate color—for example, green for bottles, red for bottle tops, and so on. When you land, pick up a card and make the noise the same number of times as the number on the card. You can make up other rules as you wish.

4	3 Miss a turn	2
5 Move four squares forward	6	7
14	13	12
15	16 Go back to start	17
24	23	22

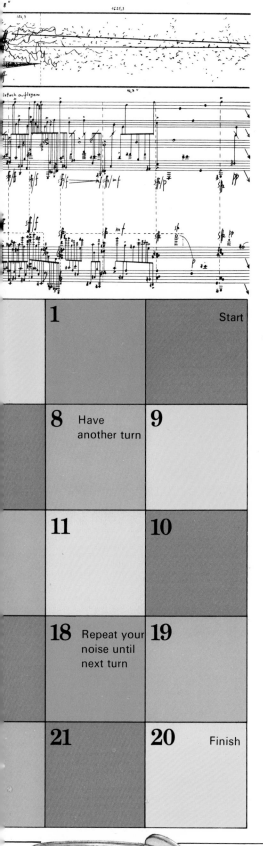

Left : A page of the performance score for Stockhausen's *Kontakte* for electronic sounds, piano and percussion. The top part between the two thick lines is a 'picture' of the electronic tape sounds. The middle band of notes is for the percussion player and the lowest band of notes is for the pianist. On this page, the pianist starts off by playing percussion as well (bottom left), but then continues on piano (bottom right). Percussion player and pianist play together, keeping in time with the electronic sounds.

1	Start
8 Have another turn	**9**
11	**10**
18 Repeat your noise until next turn	**19**
21	**20** Finish

many players do you need? You can make different patterns of sound just like a professional composer does.

Writing down sound
Then, also as a composer does, you can write your patterns down on paper to remind you how you want to play them next time. For each sound you make, invent a shape and a color in which to draw it. A bright, bell-like sound could have a clear shape on paper, a softer or a lower sound could look more like a smudge. What kind of shapes do you think your various noises make? What color is the sound of a can rattling? Once you have decided how to represent your sounds you can make up patterns on paper. Then, by reading the patterns one by one, you can play your music. Patterns on paper to represent sounds are called *scores*. Many modern composers have invented their own way of writing down sounds.

Musical games
Another way of organizing sounds is to arrange musical games. Some composers like to have surprises in their music. They make up a set of rules or instructions to players which allows them a great deal of choice of what and how to play. Because this music also has an element of chance, no two performances are ever the same. There are a number of chance elements in Karlheinz Stockhausen's music, an example of which is at the top of the page. You can invent your own games of chance using cards or dice, like the one on the left.

Musical objects
Professional composers have used many of the noises of the everyday world in their music. Giuseppe Verdi used blacksmiths' anvils in *Il Trovatore;* Richard Wagner in *The Rhinegold* did the same. Gustav Mahler used a hammer and cowbells in his *Sixth Symphony,* and George Gershwin used car horns in *An American in Paris.* Now that we can record any noise on tape, composers also use taped sounds in their music. Some even use computers to control electronic instruments and to help them compose, or they make a computer play music itself.

Keeping in time

When you were making up your music with your group of sound-makers, you probably noticed that one of the most important things to do was to decide how long each noise should last. Some sounds are much longer than others. But how can you show which is which on paper in your score?

Dividing time

If you divide your score up into equal spaces and call each space a second, or any other measure of time you like, then you can draw each sound pattern to cover as many spaces as you want it to last. Four spaces means the sound could last for the count of four or four seconds. Instead of having to watch a clock to count your beats you could have someone else beating time while you play. Musicians often use a *metronome*, a machine which can be set to make anything from one to over 200 beats a minute.

Inventing different patterns of rhythm can be fun, too. Try clapping your hands twice to each of your foot stamps. Or you could divide each beat by clapping your hands three, four or five times to each foot stamp. If you listen carefully, most music divides itself up into groups of two, three or four beats. Marching or walking music has to be in two or four time. More complicated movements such as dance steps are often in groups of three.

Different note shapes, such as half notes and whole notes, were invented in the 12th century to show the lengths of the notes compared with each other. Each note is worth two of the next. To

Above : François Couperin (1668–1733)

Whole notes
Half notes
Quarter notes
Eighth notes
Sixteenth notes

write down notes worth three of the next, shorter note, you add a dot. A dotted whole note is worth three half notes, a dotted half note three quarter notes, and

Above: Maelzel's metronome. The 'wedge' on the lever is a weight. The higher you put the weight, the slower the metronome ticks.

Right: A quarter note is worth two eighth notes. Adding a dot makes it worth three eighth notes.

Above: Although the minuet started as a country dance, it became very popular in all the courts of Europe, especially during the 18th century.

Dance patterns

Most of the instrumental music you hear is based on old dance patterns. The most important of these were developed in France in the 17th and 18th centuries. Two of the greatest composers of that time were François Couperin and Jean Philippe Rameau. Like many composers of that time, they composed groups of different types of dances called *suites*. People at court did not dance to these suites, but sat and listened to them as concert music.

One of the most important dances of the time was the *minuet*. When the French settled in America and built the city of New Orleans in the late 17th century, they took the minuet with them. There the old, stately minuet gradually became faster until it became the modern jive associated with rock and roll.

so on. As many dances have beats grouped into three this 'musical shorthand' is useful.

You can make a musical 'ruler', similar to the one above, to show how the notes relate to each other. Just as there are twelve inches to a foot, so there are a certain number of eighth notes to a quarter note, and so on.

Top: A stylized jive sequence from the musical *West Side Story*. Steady rhythms of older dances gave way to more energetic steps.

Above: A musical 'ruler'. The whole note is worth two half notes, four quarter notes, eight eighth notes, 16 sixteenth notes.

Musical codes

When you learn a tune to sing, one way of learning it is to listen to someone else play it and then try to remember it. If it is a long tune this can be quite difficult, and some music is so complicated you could not learn it in this way.

For hundreds of years, until monks invented ways of writing music in the eighth century, singers in church or court singers had to learn music by heart. As tunes became more complicated monks started to use signs called *neumes* to show whether the tune or melody went up or down, to help the memory. Soon, even this was not enough. About 300 years later musicians added a line going right across the page to show where a particular note, such as middle C, was. Once this line was drawn they started to add more and more lines until all the notes had a line or a space in between the lines. Musicians no longer guessed their notes, they had a very exact musical alphabet.

Musical alphabet
At the top of the diagram, you can see that the musical alphabet only goes up to G, then starts all over again. That is because every eighth note sounds like the first note, but eight notes higher or lower, so for that reason it can have the same name. Most music was sung at first, so the lines and spaces (or *staves*) they used covered roughly all the notes from the lowest note a man could sing to the highest a woman could. To make it clearer which was which, musicians put *clefs* at the beginning of the stave to show at what pitch the notes should be sung. The *bass clef,* developed from an old way of writing F,

shows where the F line is. The *treble clef* shows where the G line is. Musicians sometimes used a *C clef* (which shows where middle C is), halfway between the bass and treble clef, for middle voices such as tenors or altos.

Since each note was named after a letter of the alphabet, by the 16th century musicians started to use the notes to spell words, using the first seven letters of the alphabet. The words could give them an interesting tune. You can do it, too. Words such as *bed* or *cage* are easy. If you have a piano or recorder, play them and see how they sound. Some people can spell their names, can you?

Musical signatures
The German composer, Johann Sebastian Bach, could spell his name and, because he was such a famous composer, other composers

Above: At the top, piano keys are marked with their letters. Below the keyboard, the notes are on the treble (1) and bass (2) staves. First, letters A–G are used, in the normal way. Then, on the lower pair of staves, the alphabet is used.

Above: Robert Schumann (1810-1856)

B A C H

A S C H

D S C H

H A Y D N

Left: The marks painted above the words on this 14th-century manuscript are *neumes,* **an old form of writing music.**

Below: Can you decode the musical sentence at the bottom of the page? The answer is on page 45.

have used his name as the start of a piece of music in his honour.

Even though he had an H in his name, Bach could spell it because the German musical alphabet uses another letter, H, for the note we call B. The note they call B is the one we call B flat (halfway between A and B)!

Not all composers were as lucky as Bach. Another German composer, Robert Schumann, had a more difficult name to spell. However, he was lucky because the Germans also call the note E flat *Es,* so he used it as *S* because both have the same sound when pronounced. His musical letters, therefore, were *SCH*um*A*nn. Schumann liked playing musical word games. One of his girlfriends lived in a town called Asch, which had the same letters as his name. He used these letters in a piece of music called *Carnaval* as a

kind of message or secret code.

Another composer who used musical codes was the Russian Dmitri Shostakovitch. He used *S* in the same way as Schumann and got *D SCH*. These letters gave him a very individual tune which he used in much of his music as a kind of signature, similar to an artist's name on a painting.

The cleverest way to spell words in music is to give each note one of the letters of the whole alphabet. This means that an A can be H, O, V or a B an I, P, or W and so on. The French composer Maurice Ravel used this method to pay tribute to another composer, Joseph Haydn. He remembered the German way of calling *B* an *H*, which solved the problem of spelling Haydn's name in his *Minuet on the Name of Haydn.* This music was a double tribute because Haydn was a great composer of minuets, too. You can see how all these names appear in music on the left.

Your voice and music

You have read how prehistoric people probably began to use tools as instruments but, of course, their first instruments must have been their voices. The first music any person makes is by using the voice and other parts of the body, such as hands and feet. Listen carefully to anyone speaking: you will hear the voice going up and down in pitch, using higher and lower notes. Sometimes people use as many as five notes (called a fifth). Listen carefully as you speak and see how many different notes you use.

Singing simply makes more of the notes than speaking, but often makes the words stay on the same note, which is called *chanting*. Monks chant in church. This helps the words carry further, and also helps them concentrate on the meaning of the words they are chanting. Singing is much more controlled than speech. Unlike talking, singing has a very regular rhythm. Other people may often join in and enjoy making part of the group. This can happen when people sing at family celebrations, on a long bus journey, or at football games.

Folk songs

Folk songs were made up by ordinary people and passed down from generation to generation, to be sung on every kind of occasion. Now we have radio and television and people do not sing together as much as they used to. Just as all languages sound different from each other, so does the folk music of each country. This is because the song tunes have to follow the rise and fall (or *lilt*) and rhythm of speech.

Folk songs are very old tunes which have grown up with the words and have been handed

Left: Benedictine monks chanting. Monks such as these led the development of music from the 8th to the 15th century.

Above: A page from the score of Berio's *Sequenza III*. Every noise a person can make with their throat and mouth is used.

14

down by memory. Around the beginning of the 12th century in Europe, in the rich palaces of kings and princes, professional songwriters started to compose brand new songs. To begin with, they were close to folk songs in style but gradually became more and more complicated. These folk-style songs were often accepted as genuine folk songs by later generations. Examples are *Rule Britannia* in Britain, *Silent Night* and *The Linden Tree* in German-speaking countries. *The Linden Tree* was written by Franz Schubert, who was probably the greatest songwriter of all time. He died when he was only 31 but in his short lifetime wrote over 900 songs. Some, such as *The Linden Tree*, are very simple, like

folk songs, while others are very complicated, dramatic pieces.

Playing together

When you have a chance to listen to a singer accompanied by, for example, a piano, listen carefully to what the piano is playing underneath the voice part. This *accompaniment* often tells you more about the words. In Schubert's song *The Erl-King,* the piano suggests the galloping hooves of the horse as the father rushes home to try to save his son's life before the Erl-King catches him. Suddenly, the piano stops, and you know the boy is

dead. The words tell the story and the accompaniment sets the feeling or mood of the song.

Write your own song

Why not try to write a song? Make up a story about something frightening, about a storm perhaps. Then invent some sounds with the sound-makers you have collected to set a frightening or stormy mood to accompany your tune. Do not forget that your voice can also make a great many other noises such as growling, laughing and tongue-clicking. There are some modern composers who use sounds like these in their music. Luciano Berio wrote a piece of music called *Sequenza III* which uses a great many varied sounds.

Right : A Bavarian folk-singer and an accordion-player in national costume. Every country has its own distinctive style of music.

Beating sounds

On pages four and five you read how prehistoric people may have discovered music could be made by hitting one object against another. On pages eight and nine you probably found that this is the easiest way of making interesting sounds. The word *percussion,* meaning *hitting,* describes this kind of instrument. A percussion instrument can be made of metal, wood, stone or animal skin and can be hit with any kind of object.

It is fairly certain that the first instruments were percussion ones. The first element of music is rhythm and they help make rhythm clearer. Very primitive music, such as music played by the Australian aborigines, is largely rhythmic. If you listen to the music of more civilized African tribes and races you can see they have developed more complicated instruments that can play tunes as well as rhythms.

The percussion family

There are hundreds of different types of percussion instruments, but they can generally be sorted into two groups; untuned ones that do not give a particular, set note, and tuned ones that do. Then you can divide each of these groups into three further groups depending on whether they are metal (for example, bells or gongs), wood (for example, rattles) or any other natural material such as bone or stone, or skin (for example, drums). Which groups do your sound-makers belong to?

Over the centuries, basic, untuned rhythm-making percussion instruments have developed into modern, tuned,

melody-making ones, such as the xylophone. These developments show how music has moved from primitive rhythms to highly-organized sound patterns where rhythm and melody have equal importance.

The story of the drum

The first drums were probably made of hollow wood. Later, skins were stretched over hollow wooden or pottery bowls. This kind of drum would be more *resonant* (meaning the sound lasts longer and is more powerful) because skin vibrates more freely than wood. Players also found that the bigger the area of skin and the greater the depth of the bowl, the more booming the sound would be. The skin was kept tightly stretched by thongs tied round the underneath of the drum. They also found out that the tighter the thongs were, the higher the note would be. If they made different drums to play different pitches, this helped make the rhythm patterns more interesting. By pressing the thongs or the skin while they played the drums they could make the notes slide up or down a little. This kind of sound is very like the sound of the talking human voice. Many African tribes used drums to send messages.

By the 17th century in Europe,

a pair of tuned drums were regularly played with trumpets and horns in military music. When brass instruments were

Cymbals

Pedal-tuned kettledrum

Above right : The layout of a modern orchestra. The colored area shows where the percussion players are placed.

Right : These percussion instruments are used most often, but others such as xylophones, celestas and gongs can be added.

played indoors to accompany important state occasions, the kettledrums or timpani came with them. By the 1800s two or three timpani were normally used in an orchestra. Timpani players (or timpanists) could make the loud passages of music very striking by playing single, loud notes. They could also add great weight to the sound by doing a drum-roll, beating the two sticks so fast that they sounded like one, long note. When composers wanted more tuned drum notes they added more drums, until the French composer, Hector Berlioz, used 16 timpani in his *Requiem* in 1837.

The note in this kind of drum is changed by turning taps around the edge of the drum to tighten the skin or head. There are also timpani with pedals which make it easier to change the note very quickly, or even slide the note by changing it while doing a drum-roll. One of the first composers to use this sliding effect was the Hungarian Béla Bartók in his *Music for Strings, Percussion and Celesta* in 1936.

In the last 100 years, quite a few composers have used instruments such as xylophones, glockenspiels and other tuned percussion. They have used hammers, anvils, percussion instruments from the Far East, and even bottles, tea-spoons and other pieces of cutlery. Musicians who play in an orchestra call the percussion section the kitchen!

Bass drum

Hand-tuned kettledrum

Side drum

Triangle

Above : A home-made percussion band. You can make instruments like these and write music for your own group.

Keyboard music

The piano is so well-known and widely used you might think it has been around for a long time. In fact, it is one of the most recently-invented instruments. The first keyboard instruments were primitive organs, which had very simple *slides* or levers to release the notes. The first keyboards on stringed instruments appeared in the 14th century. They were little, table-top spinets or virginals and had few notes. When you press a key on one of these instruments, a small *plectrum* plucks a string inside. This explains why a virginal sounds rather like a guitar, which is plucked, too. The early keyboard instruments were also much quieter than a modern piano.

In addition to the virginal, there was another bigger instrument called a harpsichord which looks similar to a grand piano. The harpsichord was in popular use until the late 1700s. Composers such as Bach, Handel, Scarlatti, Rameau and Couperin wrote their greatest works for it.

There was another, smaller instrument in use called a clavichord. It was very quiet, too, but sensitive to touch. Bach was very fond of it. When the key is pressed it does not pluck the string as the harpsichord does. Instead there is a little blade called a *tangent* to touch the string. As long as you press the key, the tangent stays against the string.

This means you can make the note waver expressively and play it louder or softer.

The story of the piano

The piano got its name because it could also play softly (*piano* means *soft* in Italian). The first pianos, called *forte-pianos* or *loud-softs* (*forte* is Italian for *loud*) were invented around 1700. Bach played one, but at that time still preferred the clavichord. At the turn of the 19th century, the piano became more important through the music of Joseph Haydn, Wolfgang Amadeus Mozart (both from Austria) and the German composer, Ludwig van Beethoven. The piano's strings are hit, but each one is hit by a soft, felt-covered *hammer* which drops back as soon as the string has been hit. The sound continues as long as you hold the key down because another felt-covered stick called a *damper* stays away from the string until you let go, so the vibration carries on. Then, when it touches the string the sound is stopped or *damped*. Modern pianos are very powerful, with up to three strings for each note. As they became more powerful, composers wrote more and more difficult music for

pianists and sometimes tried to make the piano copy the sound of a whole orchestra. The piano's full name became *pianoforte* at the beginning of the 19th century.

Frédéric Chopin and Franz Liszt are two particularly famous composers of piano music of the 19th century. Between them they

Concert grand piano

**Above : Frédéric Chopin
(1810–1849)**

developed a way of playing the piano that cannot really be bettered. Chopin wrote hardly any music for other instruments. He created a piano style, a way of using the keyboard and a type of melody that people copied for the next 60 years. Although he lived nearly all his life away from his native Poland, Chopin always felt close to his country and wrote many pieces based on Polish dances, such as the *mazurka* and *polonaise*. His waltzes are also very popular.

Franz Liszt could not be more different from his friend Chopin. It is difficult to believe how much he crammed into his life. He travelled more, wrote more, helped other composers and was a far better performer and more original composer than most other musicians. His music is still regarded as the most difficult to play. Much of it, called *program music,* describes a person, place, picture or story. Liszt made the Hungarian style of music famous in his *Hungarian Rhapsodies.*

Harpsichord

Sounding strings

On pages four and five you saw how the idea for a harp probably developed from the early hunting bow. Other stringed instruments may have developed from a bow but all these have long, straight *necks* (which is usually where you *finger* the notes), a *body* which acts as a sound-box to make the vibrations travel further and, of course, one or more strings stretched across the whole instrument over a *bridge* and tightened by *pegs*.

You can test this way of making music yourself. Stretch a rubber band between your fingers, pluck it, and listen to the noise it makes. The thicker the band, the lower the sound; the tighter the band, the higher. If you look carefully at a stringed instrument just after you have played it, you can see the strings vibrating very fast. The vibration makes the air around the string move in waves until it comes to your ear. The shorter or tighter the cord, the faster it vibrates, and the faster or more frequently it vibrates, the higher the note.

Each musical note has its own special *frequency*. For example, the note A that you hear when an orchestra tunes up, has a frequency of 440 *cycles* or vibrations per second. If you make a string vibrate at twice that speed, or 880 cycles per second, it will be exactly one *octave* (eight notes) higher, and so on, up or down. The note an octave lower will vibrate at 220 cycles per second. Another way to raise the pitch of a note is to shorten the string by putting a finger or other kind of stop in the way; try it and see.

The string family

The commonest string instruments include the guitar

Double-bass

Above : Make your own stringed instruments. Stretch rubber bands over a cereal box (cut out a semicircle for a bridge) or stretch a string from a pole set into a wooden box to make a simple 'double-bass'.

Above : Guitarist John Williams.

Above : The double-bass is the biggest stringed instrument in the modern string family, and can play very low notes.

and the violin. The guitar was first used many centuries ago. It was brought to Spain in the ninth century from Arabia. Most guitars have six strings and a wide range of notes. Although the guitar is mainly thought of as Spanish, it has been a popular

Cello

instrument all over Europe since the 18th century, when it became more popular than the *lute* and *mandolin* (there is a lute in the smaller illustration on page 32). Many composers wrote music for it, often in combination with flute or violin. The Italian Niccolò Paganini, who perhaps was the greatest violinist there has been, was also a very good guitar player and wrote many pieces for it. Like the lute or mandolin it makes a very suitable accompaniment for a singer.

During the 15th and 16th centuries in particular, the most popular family of stringed instruments was the viol family. Although different in many ways, viols are similar in shape and size to the violin (you can see a bass viol being played on page 32) but are less powerful in sound. The viol fingerboard has ridges on it called *frets* (guitars also have frets, like those on the guitar on

the opposite page).

The violin, as we know it, first appeared in the 16th century but has very old ancestors. Gradually the violin took over from the viol, especially in Italy. Composers such as Guiseppe Tartini and Arcangelo Corelli made the best use of the expressive violins being made by people such as the famous violin-maker Stradivarius. By the middle of the 1700s the full violin family of violin, viola, cello (violoncello in full) and double-bass had almost completely taken over as the most popular group of stringed instruments.

Chamber music
In the princely courts of Europe the entertainment was given by small groups of musicians in the salons or chambers, playing *chamber music*. The most important classical chamber music was the *string quartet*, with two violins, a viola and a cello. Haydn was the great 'father' of the quartet, writing over 80 of them. He also wrote hundreds of other pieces of music for chamber groups formed with other kinds of instruments. Since then the quartet has been thought of as the most important form of chamber music a composer can write.

Viola

Violin

Above: The violoncello (or cello for short). Its notes are not quite as low as a double-bass's, and it can play quite high ones.

Above: The viola (left) is only a little bigger than the violin but has a mellower sound, and can play five notes lower.

Above: The orchestra layout showing where the string players sit (first and second violins, violas, cellos and double-basses).

Blowing in the wind

Pick up a soda bottle, or any bottle with a narrow neck-opening, and blow across the top; you will hear a quiet, humming sound. What you are doing is making the air inside vibrate against the side of the bottle. In turn, this makes the air outside vibrate and the sound waves travel to your ear. This is what happens in all wind instruments.

Good vibrations

The pitch of the note depends on the length of the column of air vibrating in the instrument, just as, on a stringed instrument, the pitch of the note depends on the length of the string. The first wind instruments were probably hollow bones, shells, gourds or pottery imitations of these. Wood became the most usual material so these instruments came to be described as *woodwind*. Soon people discovered that, if holes were made in the tube and covered in various ways with fingers, the note would change. They found out how to hollow reeds and bamboos and tune them.

Another way to get the air to vibrate is by using a *reed* in the mouthpiece of the instrument. Put a blade of grass (or paper) between your two thumbs and blow through them. You should get a very piercing sound! This is how a reed works in a woodwind instrument.

You can now divide woodwind instruments into two groups, *open flue* and *reed*. Recorders, flutes and even referees' whistles are flues; oboes, clarinets and bagpipes are reed instruments. Reeds can be *single*, as in clarinets and saxophones, or *double*, as in oboes, their big cousin, the English horn, and the bassoon.

As we have already described, stopping the holes in a wind instrument changes the length of the vibrating air column. There is another way of doing this and that is by *overblowing*. If you blow harder than you need to, the instrument will play an octave higher at double the frequency, or vibrations per second. Some instruments have holes to help you do this.

Of course, some instruments are very big and have more holes than you have fingers. Over the years, a system of keys and levers has been developed to make it easy. The standard system today was invented by Theobald Boehm in about 1830, and makes very complicated and fast passages much easier. If you can already play a recorder, it would not take you long to learn the Boehm fingering on, for example, a clarinet or bassoon.

One of the oldest instruments is the pan-pipe; you can see this on vase paintings done over 2,500 years ago. Instead of having one tube with holes in it, the pan-pipe has many tubes of different lengths bound together, one tube for each note. Pan-pipes are still very common in Rumanian folk music.

A musical genius

One of the very few composers (apart from folk musicians) to use pan-pipes was Mozart, one of the most brilliant musicians who has ever lived. He began to play the harpsichord at the age of three and compose at five and was a brilliant pianist and violinist. He knew Haydn and played quartets with him. In

Above: With all holes covered (a), the air wave is as long as the tube. In (b) and (c), shorter and more frequent waves make the notes higher.

Left : A single reed (a) and a double reed (b). There is a double reed on the bassoon. The position of the woodwind in the orchestra is shown on the right.

Bassoon

Clarinet

Oboe

Flute

Mozart's opera *The Magic Flute*, Prince Tamino is on a difficult journey to rescue Princess Pamina. Three spirits give him a magic flute to protect him and his companion Papageno some magic bells. Papageno is a bird-catcher and has a pan-pipe to help him catch the birds. He also uses the pipe to signal to Tamino when they are lost.

Make your own pan-pipe by cutting up different lengths of hollow reed or bamboo and binding them together. Blow across the tops just as you blew across the soda bottle and they will make sounds.

Left : A group or *consort* of recorders. The usual combination is, from left to right : descant, treble, tenor and bass recorders.

Above : A performance of Mozart's *The Magic Flute*. Papageno is playing his pan-pipe to catch birds. In the background is the

dead dragon that threatened the hero, Prince Tamino. Papageno pretends that he killed it, but turns out to be a coward.

Bold as brass

Brass instruments are wind instruments made of metal (not always brass); but the basic difference between brass and woodwind instruments is the mouthpiece. When you blow into a brass one, it makes your lips vibrate in the same way as the reeds of an oboe or bassoon.

Hidden notes
All brass instruments have a simple tube. Each tube produces a *series* of notes. This series varies according to the length of the tube. Every length of tube has a *fundamental note* which actually contains the sounds of the notes in its series. This is called the *harmonic series*.

The fundamental note (the first note in the series) is the *first harmonic;* the *second harmonic* (the second note) has twice as many vibrations and is an octave higher; the *third harmonic* (the third note) has three times as many vibrations and is an octave and five notes higher, the *fourth* has four times the vibrations and is two octaves higher, and so on. The higher up the series you go the closer the notes are together until, at the top, you actually get a series of notes one note apart, called a *scale*. These high notes are difficult to blow and so early brass instruments had to make do with the few notes at the bottom of the series, which do not make a complete scale. That is why a simple instrument such as the bugle plays fanfares using so few notes. Some composers, such as Bach in his second Brandenburg concerto (see page 30) have used the difficult top notes to write brilliant trumpet tunes.

In order that a brass instrument could play all the notes of the scale from the lowest to the highest, it was necessary to change the length of the tube. Then the instrument could play the harmonic series of the seven fundamentals from A to G. To lengthen the tube, extra pieces called *crooks* were added to it. Of course, this took time, so that neither trumpets nor horns played very complicated tunes until the invention of *valves*.

Making it easier
Valves have made it possible to change the length of a tube at the press of a finger. Valves for brass instruments were invented around 1800. Connected to each valve is a separate length of tube, similar to the old crook, which is added to the main tube when the valve is pressed. By using three valves in various combinations you can get all seven lengths.

Trombones have always been different. They have a *slide* which alters the length of the tube instantly. They can play any of the seven fundamental notes by

Tuba

Trumpet

Trombone

Cutaway of trumpet

Middle C

Above: Magic sounds! Press the notes marked x, y and z on a piano without making them sound, then play the one marked A and let it go.

24

Notes x, y and z will be heard quietly because they are part of the harmonic series of A. This also works in reverse.

Above: In this cutaway, you can see how air travels through the tubes of a trumpet from the mouthpiece when different notes are played.

French horn

Valve

choosing one of seven different positions for the slide. With a slide they can also make one note slide into another (a *glissando*). The tuba, which was invented in 1835, is the biggest and plays the lowest notes of the brass family.

Clever effects

Once valves had been invented, composers wrote more and more interesting music for the brass instruments. Richard Strauss was one of the most daring composers. This was not all that surprising as his father was a horn player. His *Alpine Symphony* uses 20 horns, six trumpets, six trombones and six tubas. In *Don Quixote* Strauss uses one of the strangest effects in all music to describe Don Quixote's battle with the sheep.

One of the interesting things you can do to a brass instrument is to muffle and sometimes change its tone completely with a *mute*, a sort of cone stuck into the top or bell of the tube. Strauss asks players to mute and *flutter-tongue* their instruments. The result is that they sound quite like bleating sheep! Brass instruments have a wider variety of sounds than most other instruments. By overblowing, using different mutes and flutter-tonguing they can become comic or sinister, majestic or mysterious.

The red arrows show how the air travels round when all the valves are up. The blue arrows show what happens when the valve on the right is pressed down. Air is diverted through an extra length of tube at the back, and a lower note or series of notes can be made.

Above: The position of the brass instruments in the orchestra: horns on the left, trumpets next, trombones and tubas on the right.

The orchestra

We usually know exactly what we mean when we talk about an orchestra today. It is a group of about 60 players playing all the most important instruments in the wind, brass, string and percussion families. A hundred years ago, orchestras were much smaller, and 200 years ago they were made up of whatever players were available, never more than 30. Haydn usually wrote his first orchestral music around 1750 for a small group of strings with one flute, two oboes, a bassoon and two horns. By 1790 clarinets had come to stay. In the early 1800s Beethoven added a third horn, in his third symphony, and then trombones in his fifth. More strings were now needed to balance these extra wind and brass instruments. There were between 16 and 20 violins, six to eight violas and cellos, with up to ten double-basses.

When composers such as Richard Wagner and Richard Strauss started using regularly 25 or more brass and wind instruments by the late 19th century, orchestras grew to over 100 players. Strauss's *Alpine Symphony* uses 130. It is very expensive to have such a large orchestra nowadays and composers have started writing for smaller groups. The orchestra is here to stay, though, because so much music for symphony orchestras was written between 1750 and the early 1900s. Most big towns, radio stations and opera companies have their own orchestras. Many orchestras help pay for themselves by making records and film sound-tracks as well as giving concerts.

The instruments

The strings are the main group of instruments. The string players sit in front of the louder instruments, divided into two groups. The first violins usually play the important tunes, but sometimes change with the second violins sitting behind or opposite them. The *leader* of the first violins (concertmaster) leads the whole orchestra and is almost as important as the conductor. The violas play the middle harmonies with the second violins, and the cellos play the bass notes. The double-basses usually play the same notes as the cellos, but an octave lower.

The woodwinds sit in the middle of the orchestra with the instruments that play the highest notes, the flutes, on the left. The

Piano (Soft)   Pizzicato (Plucked)   Dolce (Sweetly)

Above center: The layout of a modern orchestra often looks like this but may vary. Percussion players also often play more than one instrument.

- Harpist
- Concertmaster
- First violins
- Second violins
- Violas
- Cellos
- Double-basses
- Flutes

Molto Doloroso
(Very sadly)

Con forza
(Forcefully)

brass sit behind the woodwinds and, the noisiest of all, the percussion are right at the back.

The conductor

With so many musicians to keep together, orchestras usually have someone to beat time in front of them. Two hundred years ago, the conductor also played the violin or the harpsichord with the orchestra but, as music became more and more complicated, they had to concentrate on directing the other musicians. As well as keeping time, starting and stopping the players together, reminding them to go slower or faster as the composer requires, a conductor also interprets the music. He tells the players how he thinks the composer wanted it to sound (words such as those on the left are written over the music), and listens carefully to the balance of the instruments. The conductor even shows them the best way of playing a tricky passage and tries to inspire them with the mood of the piece. Conductors have to have exceptionally good hearing and usually have worked in orchestras before they start to direct them. Sometimes, though, conductors start conducting right from the start. The best conductors can usually learn by heart the music for all the instruments playing a piece of music.

Beating time

Beating time is quite simple; look at the diagrams and see how to beat two, three or four beats to a bar. Depending on where

Two beats to the bar

Three beats to the bar

Four beats to the bar

the conductor's hand is, the players can tell what beat of the bar they should be on. If he makes large moves, this is a signal for the musicians to get louder, if he makes little ones they play more quietly. Try conducting for yourself. Any music on a record, cassette or the radio will do.

◻ Oboes
◻ Clarinets
◻ Bassoons
◻ Horns

◻ Trumpets
◻ Trombones
◻ Tubas
◻ Percussion

The symphony

The word *symphony* simply means *sounding together*. For 200 years, from about 1750, the most important piece of music a composer could write was a symphony. Orchestras are called *symphony orchestras* because originally they were developed to cope with the kind of music composers were writing in their symphonies. What is a symphony and how did it begin? The story of the symphony starts when operas—dramatic stories set to music—were first becoming popular. For opera composers in the 17th and 18th centuries, a symphony was any piece of instrumental music played between the sung parts of the opera, but especially the music at the beginning, now called an *overture*.

In Italy, overtures had three sections: a fast, catchy one to begin with, then a slower one and often a fast, last one. Sometimes this last one would be a minuet. The three sections of the overture soon split off from each other and became completely separate *movements*. Gradually symphonies (or overtures as they were often still called) settled down to a regular four-movement pattern. There was a fast, first movement, a slow second, a minuet for the third movement and a fast finale.

Great symphony writers

Haydn was the first great composer of symphonies. Mozart followed his example and Beethoven learned from them both. All three composers happened to be living in Vienna (a famous center for music) at about the same time. Ever since then, the most important symphonists have worked there, including Franz Schubert, Johannes Brahms, Anton Bruckner and Gustav Mahler.

It was Beethoven, though, who showed what symphonies could really do. He made his symphonies express the great excitement people were feeling at the time when the French revolution seemed to be promising freedom to so many people. He even dedicated his third symphony to Napoleon but, when he heard Napoleon had crowned himself emperor, he tore up the page. It still sounds a heroic symphony though, and is called the *Eroica* (or *Heroic*) *Symphony*. Most symphonies are not meant to describe any person or event. Those which do are usually called *symphonic poems*. Richard Strauss's *Alpine Symphony* and *Don Quixote*, mentioned on pages 24 and 25, are really two of these.

The shape of a symphony

A symphony is very like a play: it is a drama in music, a play of great musical ideas. Most of the drama goes on in the first movement, which is designed in a special way, called *sonata form*. The two basic shapes at the beginning are brought into close contact in the middle and then everything is brought back into order by the end. The two patterns stand for two tunes or *themes* which are brought together in the middle of a symphony in a series of more complicated musical ideas – similar to two characters arguing with each other in a play.

Above: A detail from David's painting of the coronation of Napoleon. Napoleon is seen crowning his Empress Josephine.

Two of Beethoven's most famous symphonies, his third and fifth, show this pattern very clearly. They all start with a bold first tune, called the *first subject*.

Then there is a contrasting group of tunes called the *second subject*. The middle section, where the tunes are brought together, is called a *development*,

because the composer tries his themes out to see how he can make them change or develop, suggest other ideas and add to the excitement. The last section, in which the first and second subjects are repeated in the form they were in at the start, is called the *recapitulation*. Beethoven's fifth symphony is the clearest. The very famous first four notes really give the composer all he needs. He builds those notes up into a strong first subject and even uses the same rhythm on the horns to start the second one. As a complete contrast, the second movement is slow and song-like. In this symphony, though, Beethoven turns the minuet into a movement so fast you couldn't possibly dance to it! This is called a *scherzo*, which is designed to get the pulses racing again. The finale keeps up the pace, but Beethoven often uses the same design as the first movement to end a symphony at a high level of dramatic excitement.

First subject   Second subject   Development   Recapitulation

Above: A diagram of the first movement of a symphony or sonata.

Above: The first page of Beethoven's *Symphony No 5*. There is a line for each instrument. Notice how the score starts with some of the woodwinds, then the brass, timpani and strings. Can you see the shape of the famous opening tune?

Above: Ludwig van Beethoven (1770-1827) carried notebooks around to 'sketch' tunes to work on at a later date.

29

Building patterns

On pages 28 and 29 you read about music which does not imitate or describe anything directly. When you listen to it, pictures might come into your head but the composers were usually just thinking of the sounds when they wrote the music. This kind of music is called *abstract music*. There are also abstract paintings. Just as an abstract painter builds up patterns of shape and color on a canvas, so an abstract composer builds patterns of notes and instrumental color in his music.

When Johann Sebastian Bach was writing music, about 250 years ago, people admired elegant style and pattern. Buildings, particularly churches, were decorated with very complicated designs. Organs in the churches were built with careful attention to the balance of pipework. In the photograph (right) you can see how all the ranks of pipes are grouped into intricate patterns.

Patterns in music
Similar patterns were reflected in the music of the time. At the bottom of the page is part of the *Toccata and Fugue in D Minor* by Bach. The composer makes a striking start to the toccata: the first note with the sign above it is a high, loud 'twiddle' which catches our attention, and makes us wait eagerly for what follows. The run of short, fast notes that comes next is a surprising contrast. Bach then repeats the pattern at a lower pitch, slightly altering it, as well. Then Bach builds a new line made up of a new pattern. This kind of thing happens all the way through the toccata.

Toccata is the Italian word for *touched,* and is a piece in which players can show how well they can play or their skill of touch.

A *fugue* is another kind of musical pattern-making. It starts with a tune called the *subject*. Then, as in a round such as *Frère Jacques*, another voice or instrument (or on keyboard instruments, another hand) takes up the subject, and the first voice builds up patterns around it.

The concerto
Musical patterns can sound very exciting, when the composer juggles with high and low notes, long or short notes or groups of notes. Instruments can play against each other or a solo melody can be contrasted against another played with many instruments blending with one another. This is the basis of *concerto* form. A concerto in Bach's day played off different groups of instruments against each other as well as showing them off as solo instruments. In the beginning of the score of Bach's second Brandenburg concerto the notes, put together, form different shapes, and the tune is built up of groups of these shapes. The notes are like bricks making patterns in a wall. The trumpet's notes make up one wall of a house, which is added to by

each of the other instruments, so that the whole piece of music can be thought of as a building.

Since about 1918, composers have been writing abstract music again. The Russian, Igor Stravinsky, and the German, Paul Hindemith, are the most important composers of this kind of music.

Serial music
A different type of pattern-making was invented by Arnold Schoenberg. He organized the 12 semi-tones of the octave into a

Above: Johann Sebastian Bach (1685-1750)

Right: The beginning of Bach's *Toccata and Fugue in D minor.* **Can you work out the boy's expressions as he listens to it?**

series, which then formed the
basis for a whole composition.
This is called *serial music*, or
sometimes *12-tone music*. Often
the music is built up of little cells
of notes, such as his piano pieces
written in 1909.

Right : The 18th-century organ in
Göttweig Abbey, Austria.
Instruments such as this show the
same balanced design as the music
written for them. Each group of
pipes is controlled by a *stop* and
each rank of pipes makes a different
quality of sound in the same way as
instruments in an orchestra.

**Above : Arnold Schoenberg
(1874-1951)**

Singing together

You have read how important it was for people to sing. Many people like singing in groups; large groups such as choirs or small ones such as barber-shop quartets or the groups that used to gather round the piano in Victorian parlors. In the princely households of the 15th, 16th and 17th centuries the most important form of group vocal music was the *madrigal*. This could be sung by any number of singers from two to ten, with or without the accompaniment of lutes or viols. The songs were usually love poems but often also descriptions of hunts or battles. The music often took its cue from the words and imitated hunting horns, bird calls or street cries. Sometimes the music illustrated words such as *fall, flowing river* or *mountains*, by making the notes drop down, flow smoothly or rise up and down. The English *madrigalists* learnt their art from the Italians. Englishmen such as William Byrd and Orlando Gibbons raised it to a high peak.

Splendid masques

Meanwhile men such as Claudio Monteverdi in Italy were starting new kinds of songwriting. Another development of the madrigal in Italy was to string a series of them together to tell a story. This *madrigal comedy* was acted out, and eventually led to the first operas appearing around 1600. Musical stories were also told in the form of a *masque* in many courts in Europe. In a masque, the whole court danced, sang and acted out a well-known story or myth from ancient history. Gradually masques were brought in as interludes in theatrical presentations.

Henry Purcell was one of the greatest composers of such works. His own teacher, John Blow, gave up his position as organist of Westminster Abbey for him. Purcell's vocal music has for long been regarded as the greatest example of setting words to music in English, the art of finding the most suitable rhythm or melodies to match the meaning and expression of a word. Purcell composed the first real English opera, called *Dido and Aeneas*, for a girl's school.

Songs of praise

By the time the great composer George Frederick Handel settled in London Purcell was dead,

Above : Making music in the 17th century. The lady in the middle is playing a lute, the man on the right a bass viol, while the others sing.

Right : A courtly masque at an Elizabethan wedding. The musicians are playing a flute (left) and a viol (right).

but Handel was still greatly influenced by Purcell's music. Handel wrote many pieces of music for the large choirs in English churches and courts. Although he came to England as an opera composer he began to compose a whole series of *oratorios* to be performed during Lent, when the Church did not allow operas to be performed. An oratorio tells a story, usually on a religious subject, but it is not acted in the same way as an opera. The most famous oratorio is Handel's *Messiah*.

For the 250 years since Handel's day, oratorio has been a very important form in English music. Later composers were inspired by Handel's example to compose some of their greatest works after visiting England, where nearly every town had its choral society as well as its orchestra. Haydn wrote *The Creation* and *The Seasons*, and Mendelssohn wrote *Elijah*. Edward Elgar gave the oratorio a new lease of life in Britain in the 1900s with works such as *The Dream of Gerontius* and *The Apostles*. Later, Benjamin Britten developed British choral music, but usually for smaller groups than the 200 singers needed in a 19th-century oratorio. Britten was greatly influenced by Purcell, and his *Young Persons' Guide to the Orchestra* is based on a theme from a Purcell dance. He wrote several pieces to be performed in church, some for children such as *Noye's Fludde*. Others, called *Parables for Church Performance*, imitate Japanese plays. He also wrote many operas.

Above : George Frederic Handel (1685–1759) dominated music in London for 40 years and influenced English music for about 100 years.

Singing a story

The word *opera* covers many different styles of music. The one thing they all have in common is a story, acted out on stage by singers accompanied by a group of instrumentalists. Operas can be short and simple, or they can be very long and complicated. Large operas need huge orchestras, choruses, many singers and dancers and large stages with a great deal of scenery and technicians to operate it. Some operas are sung all the way through; in others characters speak between the songs.

Opera began in Italy around 1600. Monteverdi was the first great opera composer. By the 1700s there were two basic styles in Italy, *seria* or serious opera, and *buffa* or comic opera. Handel wrote in the seria style, but by the end of the century Mozart had brought the two styles together. His operas, such as *The Marriage of Figaro* and *Don Giovanni,* have both serious and comic elements. Another style that was developed in France and Germany was the *Singspiel* or *sungplay.* In this spoken dialogue is used between songs. *The Magic Flute*, Mozart's last opera, and *Fidelio,* Beethoven's only one, are in this style.

Musical mascots

In the 19th century the opera world split into two camps, the Italian one led by Giuseppe Verdi and the German one led by Richard Wagner. The Italians developed the art of singing, and wrote music that was designed to show off the voice. The Germans wrote *symphonic* operas, where the music was composed with the same principles of development as a symphony. The split in the opera world was wide because Italian nationalists adopted Verdi as a mascot, while Wagner was heavily involved in politics and revolution in Germany.

The Italians scrawled Verdi's name on walls as a code because it stood for *V*ictor *E*manuel *R*e *d'I*talia, the king who they hoped would unite Italy and throw out foreign rulers. Verdi was born in 1813, the same year as Wagner. One of his most famous operas is *Aida*, which tells the story of an Ethiopian princess who falls in love with an Egyptian general.

Out of love for her he betrays the Egyptian army and is buried alive with her under a pyramid. *Aida* was written to celebrate the opening of the Suez Canal and was first performed in Cairo. There is a famous triumphal march in *Aida* which needs many singers and dancers.

The story of The Ring

Wagner also wrote at a time when all the German states were beginning to feel the need to unite. Four of his operas are intended to be performed as a series. They tell the old, mythological story of the *Ring*

Above : Giuseppe Verdi (1813–1901)

Above : Richard Wagner (1813–1883)

Left : As the three Norns weave the thread of fate at the beginning of *The Twilight of the Gods,* it breaks and they know the end of the old world is near.

of the Nibelung. The Ring is made from Gold, stolen from the bottom of the Rhine by the dwarf Alberich. He hopes to rule the world with its power but Wotan, king of the gods, creates a race of heroes to conquer him and bring a new era of justice. This was Wagner's way of criticizing the evils he saw around him.

There is plenty of action in the fourth and last opera, *The Twilight of the Gods.* The hero, Siegfried, is drugged into betraying his love, Brunhilde, by Alberich's son, Hagen, and wants to marry another woman. When Siegfried realises what has happened, Hagen kills him and tries to steal the Ring for himself. Brunhilde stops him and throws herself on to Siegfried's funeral pyre. The waters of the Rhine well up and, destroying the old world, win back the Ring.

Not many operas need as many people to perform them as *Aida* or *The Ring.* Mozart's operas, such as *The Magic Flute* which is described on page 23, use smaller orchestras. Most of Handel's operas have no chorus. Modern composers, such as Benjamin Britten (see page 33), have written for smaller numbers of performers than Verdi or Wagner. These operas can be performed quite cheaply, and do not have to be put on in big theatres. They can be produced anywhere where there is enough space for performers and audience.

Left : Radames, the Egyptian general, arrives at the Pharoah's court after his victory over the Ethiopians in *Aida.*

Dancing a story

Dance has always been associated with France. Elegant dances were developed at the French court in the middle of the 17th century. French opera also always had an important element of ballet. That is why most ballet terms are in French. By the middle of the 19th century, though, Russia had become the center of dance, and this continued right into the middle of the 20th century. Two composers, Pyotr Ilyich Tchaikovsky and Igor Stravinsky, are particularly associated with the history of ballet over the last hundred years.

The start of modern ballet
The three ballet scores of Tchaikovsky, *Sleeping Beauty, Swan Lake* and *Nutcracker,* are undoubtedly the most popular ever written. His rich melody and brilliant use of the orchestra seem to match the magic and mysterious stories of the ballets. Russian music in general had not made a great impact before Tchaikovsky, but after him a whole new group of brilliant composers developed.

Left : Pyotr Ilyich Tchaikovsky (1840–1893)

Above : A scene from a performance of Tchaikovsky's last ballet, *The Nutcracker*. This ballet tells the story of a nutcracker given as a present to a girl, Clara. Clara dreams that the nutcracker turns into a prince who takes her on a fabulous journey. These dancers are 'snowflakes' that they meet in the Land of Snow on the way to their journey's end.

Tchaikovsky also wrote many operas, some such as *Eugene Onegin* with famous dance scenes. He wrote many symphonies as well but even these sound at times like ballet scores.

Just as in opera, the main action of a ballet story is danced by solo dancers in the character parts. There is also a *corps de ballet*, the dance equivalent of the chorus in an opera, who usually take the part of crowds, courtiers, armies and servants. Just as most large cities have their own choral society and orchestra, they often have a ballet company.

Brilliant partners

Early in the 20th century, the Russian impresario Serge Diaghilev travelled Europe with a Russian ballet company. He invited Igor Stravinsky to write some music for a new ballet, *The Firebird*. Stravinsky's first three ballets, *The Firebird, Petrushka* and *The Rite of Spring,* are not danced very often because of their extreme difficulty, but their music is among his most popular. There was a riot at the first performance of *The Rite of Spring.* The audience was outraged by what it considered Stravinsky's

discordant harmonies and jagged rhythms. These describe a pagan ceremony when a young girl dances herself to death to make the land give a good harvest.

The Firebird

The Firebird was more acceptable, and remains one of Stravinsky's richest scores. It tells the story of the Firebird who gives the Prince one of her feathers to call her when he is in danger. The Prince uses the feather to call the Firebird to help him rescue the Tsar's daughter, whom he then marries. Stravinsky wrote many other ballets. One of them, *The Fairy's Kiss,* is based on melodies by Tchaikovsky. Like Tchaikovsky, Stravinsky also wrote symphonies, and these, too, sound like ballet scores. Stravinsky wrote 12 important ballets in his life. During that time, he was regarded as the most important composer of the century.

Above : A scene from *The Firebird* by Stravinsky. Prince Ivan has captured the Firebird and only lets her go when she gives him one of her feathers. The music she dances to, and the choreography, or dance design, make her seem almost like a real bird.

Above : Igor Stravinsky (1882-1971) His ballet music is so interesting it is often played in concerts without dancers.

Musical backcloths

Music plays another important part in the theatre beside ballet and opera. Many straight plays need music at some time or another. It helps put an audience in the right mood by suggesting the atmosphere of a scene of action, such as night or a storm. It can break the mood of one scene to get into another, and cover up long and difficult scene changes so that an audience remains in the right frame of mind. Quite often there are songs, too, which need instrumental accompaniment. This kind of music is called *incidental* music.

Music for plays

Nowadays most incidental music is recorded and played on discs or tapes, but quite a few of the larger theaters hire small groups of musicians for their plays, especially if there is much singing. In earlier times, though, most theaters had their own orchestras. The incidental music Felix Mendelssohn wrote for a production of Shakespeare's *A Midsummer Night's Dream* is where the famous *Wedding March* comes from. At the top of the next page you can see the fairy queen and attendants in a scene from the play. Beethoven's music for *Egmont* by Goethe needed a full symphony orchestra and a chorus, and is regarded as a very important part of the composer's work.

When composers wrote for plays they usually composed a full-scale overture just as for an opera. Then they wrote various pieces, called *intermezzos*, to go between the scenes and *entr'actes,* between the acts. If music was needed to accompany speech it was called a *melodrama.* Some of the most popular music by many composers has been written as incidental music for plays, and is often the only reason some plays are remembered. Music such as that which Franz Schubert wrote for *Rosamunde,* Frederick Delius for *Hassan* and Ralph Vaughan Williams for *The Wasps* are examples.

The story of Peer Gynt

Perhaps the most famous incidental music ever written was that which Edvard Grieg wrote for Ibsen's play *Peer Gynt*, and includes *In the Hall of the Mountain King.* Ibsen's play is already a very long one, but it would last nearly nine hours with all Grieg's music. It tells of the wanderings of Peer Gynt throughout the world in search of love and adventure, before returning home, a wiser man, to die in the arms of Solveig, the woman who had always loved him.

Music for Finland

Another composer from northern Europe who actually wrote more incidental music than anyone since Purcell, is the Finnish composer Jean Sibelius. His *Karelia* music was among his earliest and remains his most popular. He also wrote some music for a production of Shakespeare's *The Tempest*. This begins with a very realistic orchestral description of a storm. Right from the start, Sibelius set out to give his country music to be proud of. He was as nationalistic as Grieg, Liszt, Chopin, Bartók or Elgar.

Above: Edvard Grieg (1843-1907) was a fine pianist and his piano concerto is one of the most popular there is.

Above: A typical scene of the countryside in Finland, very like the landscape of Karelia which inspired Sibelius.

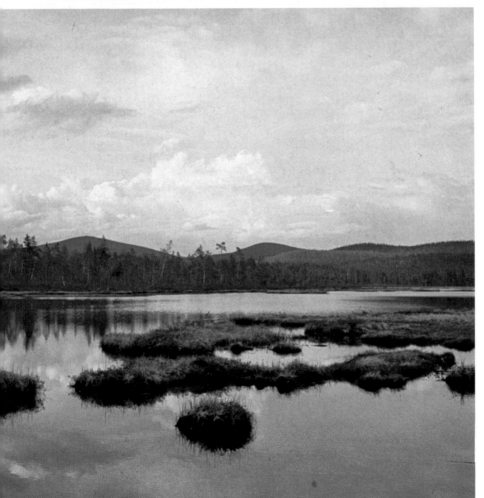

**Above : Jean Sibelius
(1865-1957)**

**Above left : Titania, the fairy queen,
in** *A Midsummer Night's Dream.*

Karelia is a province of South
Finland, and many of his other
pieces are symphonic poems
describing stories from Finnish
folklore, such as the *Swan of
Tuonela,* or the *Lemminkäinen
Legends.* Even his abstract
symphonies seem to have the
atmosphere of the calm Finnish
landscape of lakes and forests.

Film music

Another branch of incidental
music that has taken over from
theatrical music is film music.
Film producers may often have
the money to pay for large
orchestras to play film music.
Although, in general, music
written for films is not as
important as much of the music
you have just read about, film
music does provide one of the
main ways in which composers
and orchestras can earn a living
today.

Musical suggestions

Sibelius's prelude to *The Tempest* suggests a storm at sea. The movement of the notes, the busy rise and fall, the thickness of the sound, the dark and shrill color of the instruments Sibelius uses, all give an unmistakable impression of a storm.

Imitating real sounds

Music can imitate natural things such as bells, cow-horns or bird-calls almost exactly. Composers can also use recordings of everyday sounds to color their music. For the hundreds of years before tape recorders were invented, though, musicians enjoyed trying to imitate such things as sea-battles, storms and hunts. The German composer Johann Kuhnau, told the story of David and Goliath in one of his *Biblical Sonatas.* People enjoyed listening to the clever way the composer used various instruments to imitate the sounds of the battle that takes place between the hero David and the giant Goliath.

Program music, as it is called, was always an important part of French music. In their keyboard music, Couperin and Rameau invented a great deal of fanciful titles for each movement, such as *Les Tricoteuses (The Knitting Women)* or *Les Barricades Mystérieuses (The Mysterious Barricades).* By the time Debussy and Ravel were writing music, around 200 years later, Berlioz, Liszt and Strauss had all made brave attempts to write program music describing everything from a Witches' Sabbath to St Francis Walking on the Waters or Don Quixote Fighting Sheep.

The color of sound

Debussy, though, had a fine appreciation of sound for its own sake, just as impressionist painters were more interested in light than the objects it helped them to see. Much impressionist music simply describes pictures or scenes, but most of Debussy's music just uses the title of a piece as a starting point for interesting musical explorations of sounds for their own sakes. The development of the piano had a lot to do with it. It had become an adaptable, expressive instrument that could conjure up worlds of magical sound. It was almost as if different *chords,* or combinations of notes, had a color and meaning of their own. See if you can create different-colored sounds by experimenting on a keyboard. Watery effects are easy to get, but you can also make brilliant, bright chords or short, sharp, jagged ones, warm or somber ones that are dark in color. What colors do your sounds suggest?

Above right : Claude Debussy (1862–1918) put a great deal of very careful work into creating a certain impression or feeling in his music.

a

Middle C

b

Middle C

Above: Try playing these chords together, first (a) then (b). What ideas or colors do the sounds put into your head? Does the first chord sound more pleasant?

Write the notes down and label the sounds they suggest. Some composers even link different notes with different colors.

Water music

Water features very often in impressionist music. The piano can so easily suggest rain, fountains or rivers. In *La Cathédrale Engloutie* (*The Submerged Cathedral*), Debussy suggests a wonderful scene of a cathedral sunk in the sea, the bells tolling with the movements of the waves, and a ghostly choir

Left: Part of the score of Debussy's *La Mer*. Even the notes suggest waves.

still singing. He does this by using wide chords at the top and bottom of the keyboard.

He also wrote a well-known orchestral piece of water music called *La Mer* (*The Sea*). It is very interesting to compare the way he uses the instruments with what Sibelius does in *The Tempest*. With detailed directions to the players, Debussy builds up a picture of dawn at sea. The gulls, swooping over the waves, are suggested by the wind instruments. Quiet cymbal clashes suggest the wind catching the foam from the wave tops, and the solemn brass chords suggest the powerful movement of the tide.

Another famous French impressionist was Maurice Ravel. One of his first pieces of music was a water piece, *Jeux d'Eaux* (*The Fountains*). This is a brilliant description of a fountain interpreted by a piano. It was inspired by a similar piece of music by Liszt called *Les Jeux d'Eaux à la Villa d'Este* (*Fountains at the Villa d'Este*).

Masters of music

As you read at the beginning of the book, anybody can write some kind of music and many do. Only a few composers, though, have done it so well and so differently that they catch people's imaginations and make them wonder what the world could have been like without such music. Each composer, in his or her own way, has developed the way we listen, the way we think and feel, and how we act in our daily lives. Each important composer has made a major contribution to at least one form of music: opera, ballet, chamber or piano music, song, the symphony, choral music – all the various types of music that you have read about. Hundreds of composers have inspired millions of people over the centuries; these, together with others whom you have read about in the book, are a few of the composers who have played an important part in the story of music.

The composers pictured here and in the rest of *Looking at Music* span over 400 years of musical history. Music has changed a great deal in that period. In William Byrd's day most people had a clear idea of what they thought music was— it would not have included anything Karlheinz Stockhausen calls music today, but then they did not have electronics. New instruments mean new sounds which, in turn, mean new methods of composing and new music. New but not better. Each of these men, in his own way, wrote the best music of its type. They all kept their ears and minds open, and thought about what they heard. You can, too!

William Byrd
(c. 1542–1623)

Henry Purcell
(1659–1695)

Johannes Brahms
(1833–1897)

Franz Liszt
(1811–1886)

Benjamin Britten
(1913–1976)

Jean Philippe Rameau
(1683–1764)

Wolfgang Amadeus Mozart
(1756–1791)

Franz Schubert
(1797–1828)

Richard Strauss
(1864–1949)

Maurice Ravel
(1875–1937)

Béla Bartók
(1881–1945)

Karlheinz Stockhausen
(b. 1928)

What to do next

This book can only show you the tip of the musical iceberg. There is much more to discover and many ways of doing it. More people take part in musical activities than in anything else except sport. Even if you are not particularly musical or do not want to become a professional musician, you can get a great deal out of joining a choir or instrumental group such as a recorder consort or an orchestra. Do not forget, too, that anyone can compose!

You may be more interested in playing a solo instrument, or in accompanying a singer or instrumental soloist. Or you might just like to listen. If you join a music club, you can often get cheap tickets to concerts, or have expert musicians come and talk to your group. Clubs exist, also, for opera and ballet lovers, and they can often organize visits to the

backstage area of a theatre and to dress rehearsals of operas and ballets.

Learning to play
If you want to learn an instrument, you can usually do it at school. If your school does not have the instrument you want, your music teacher can often help to arrange to rent the instrument for you and provide special lessons.

Many of the schools have their own orchestras, and also put on frequent performances of children's operas. If you're very enthusiastic you can go on special musical holidays, where you can sing or play in a group or just listen to the music.

To become a professional musician you generally need to have had some experience of music-making, either playing, singing or composing, to have